Carl Maria von
WEBER

ANDANTE E RONDO ONGARESE
Op. 35

Edited by
Richard W. Sargeant, Jr.

Study Score
Partitur

SERENISSIMA MUSIC, INC.

ORCHESTRA

2 Flutes

2 Oboes

2 Bassoons

4 Horns (F)*

2 Trumpets (C)

Timpani

Violin I

Violin II

Viola

Violoncello

Double Bass

*The present score has been updated for the commonkeys of modern instruments
(Clarinets in A or B-flat, Horns in F, Trumpets in C).
The composer's original score featured Horns in C.

Duration: ca. 10 minutes

Premiere: February 19, 1813
Prague, Georg Friedrich Brandt (bassoon solo)

ISMN: 979-0-58042-125-8
This score is a newly engraved urtext edition prepared
from the primary sources.

Printed in the USA
First Printing: August, 2018

ANDANTE E RONDO UNGARESE
for Bassoon and Orchestra
Op. 35

Carl Maria von Weber
Edited by Richard W. Sargeant, Jr.

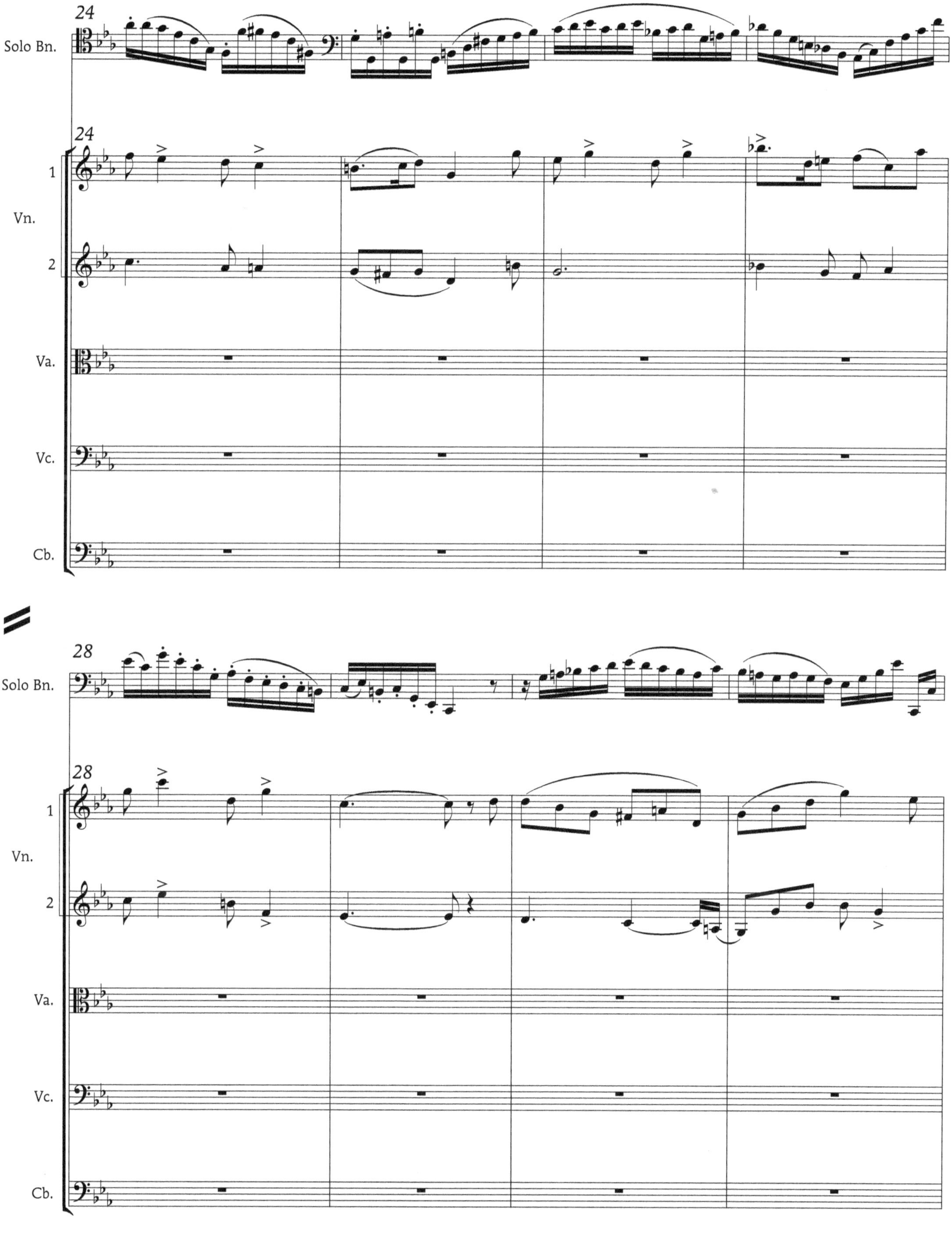
24
Solo Bn.
24
Vn.
1
2
Va.
Vc.
Cb.
28
Solo Bn.
28
Vn.
1
2
Va.
Vc.
Cb.

14

16

18

36

54